AT HOME IN WORLD WAR TWO

THE BLITZ

Stewart Ross

IMPERIAL WAR
MUSEUM

Evans

Evans Brothers Limited

The blitz

Published by Evans Brothers Limited
2A Portman Mansions
Chiltern Street
London. W1U 6NR
First Published 2002. Reprinted 2003, 2004, 2005.
© White-Thomson Publishing Limited 2002

Produced for Evans Brothers Limited by
White-Thomson Publishing Ltd.
2/3 St Andrew's Place
Lewes East Sussex BN7 1UP

Printed in Dubai

Editor: Philippa Smith
Consultant: Terry Charman, Historian, Research and Information Department, Imperial War Museum
Designer: Christopher Halls, Mind's Eye Design, Lewes
Proofreader: Alison Cooper

British Library Cataloguing in Publication Data
Ross, Stewart
  The blitz. - (At home in World War Two)
  1. World War, 1939-1945 - Campaigns - Great Britain 2. World War, 1939-1945 - Aerial operations, German 3. Great Britain - History - Bombardment, 1944-1945
  I. Title
  941'.084
ISBN: 0 237 52304 3

Captions:
Cover and this page: A Government poster encouraging everyone to help defeat the menace of enemy firebombs. 'Fritz' was a slang word for a German.
Cover (centre): An air-raid warden looks after a little girl after a V1 had destroyed her home in 1944.
Cover (background): Firefighters battling with a blaze during the London Blitz.
Title page: Standing in front of a bomb-damaged house, a group of children from Battersea, London, celebrate VE (Victory in Europe) Day, 8 May 1945.
Contents page: An air-raid warden's equipment: identity card, ration book, torch, whistle, armband and gas mask (which covered the eyes, nose and mouth in case poison gas bombs were dropped).
Acknowledgement: The author would like to thank Tom Holloway and Alan Putland for permission to use material from their websites.
For sources of quoted material see page 31.

VISIT OUR WEBSITE
Evans
www.evansbooks.co.uk

CONTENTS

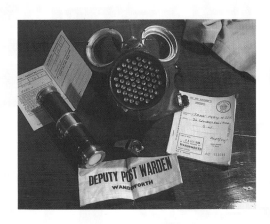

THE HOME FRONT

Britain joined World War Two in September 1939 when it declared war on Germany. France, Belgium, the Netherlands, Poland and other countries fought with Britain against Germany and, later, against Italy. In 1941, the USSR and the USA joined the war on the same side as Britain. Japan joined the side of Germany and Italy. This spread the fighting right round the world. The war finally ended in 1945.

▲ *The news everyone had feared – a newspaper poster of 3 September 1939 announces the start of World War Two in Britain.*

The fighting in World War Two took place on land, at sea and in the air. Although aircraft had been used previously in World War One (1914–18), this was the first big war in which aircraft played such an important part. There were two main types of plane. Bombers were large, slow planes that flew long distances and dropped bombs on the enemy. Fighters were small, fast planes that tried to shoot down bombers.

THE PATH TO WAR

Adolf Hitler became leader of Germany in 1933. Backed by his Nazi Party, he removed those who were against him and began taking over neighbouring countries. After Germany took over Czechoslovakia, Britain and France promised other countries that they would oppose Nazi aggression if the Germans attacked anyone else. On 1 September 1939 Hitler invaded Poland. Two days later, Britain and France declared war on Germany.

◄ *Adolf Hitler, the German leader who wanted to make his country the 'master of Europe'. The men beside him are raising their hands in a straight-arm Nazi salute.*

German bombers flew to Britain and dropped bombs on towns and cities. The British bombed German towns and cities, too. Because of air raids, no one could escape the war. Everyone's home might be in the 'front line'. That is why we say the war was fought on the 'Home Front' as well as the battle front.

The Germans invented a new type of war called *Blitzkrieg*. It means 'lightning war'. *Blitzkrieg* was attacking the enemy very quickly and hard with lots of soldiers, tanks and planes.

The British changed the meaning of *Blitzkrieg*. To them it meant a bombing attack on a town or city. They also shortened the word to 'Blitz'. The most famous Blitz was the London Blitz of 1940–41.

THE LONDON BLITZ

The London Blitz began on 7 September 1940 and lasted until May 1941. London was bombed less often after that.

Doreen Wilkinson remembers very clearly living in London during the Blitz.

'I was almost 18 when the Blitz started. Do you know what I remember most? It was the noises. The air-raid sirens, the bang! bang! of the guns, the thump! thump! of the bombs, the bells on the fire engines and ambulances.

For two years I worked in a Rest and Information Centre. That was where people came after a raid for first aid, news or just a cup of tea. I worked on information. Some lady might come up to me and ask, "Can you tell me about Kimberley Street? My mum lives there and they say it's been hit."

Then I would look up Kimberley Street and have to tell her, "Numbers 6–20 got a direct hit. No survivors. Other side of street damaged. Two believed killed. Five people taken to St Mary's Hospital." I would hope her mum was OK, but there was no way of telling.'

The first attacks came in daylight. It was quite easy to see the bombers and to try to shoot them down. Later, raids were made only at night. At the height of the Blitz London was bombed on 57 nights in a row.

▶ *Two German Dornier bombers flying over London in 1940.*

▼ *London's dock area burns after a heavy daylight bombing raid on 7 September 1940.*

Many attacks were aimed at the docks, where ships arrived with food and supplies. But it was difficult to aim in the dark, so bombs fell all over the city. They destroyed more than a million London homes, like the ones in Kimberley Street.

In the *News Chronicle* of 31 May 1941 A.J. Cummings explained what he thought was the effect of the Blitz on London:

> 'These attempts to "erase" the metropolis (to quote the Führer's own word) have filled the population with a cold and bitter resolve. There will be no peace for the Nazis now but the peace of death.'

▶ *Where shall we live now? Londoners gather after a raid that has destroyed their homes. There is a bombed-out building in the background.*

'I believe I shall feel prouder and stronger all my life for having been so tested.'

From the diary of Mrs Rosemary Black, a wealthy widow who lived in St John's Wood, London, with her two children

◀ *A woman air-raid warden tries to comfort a little girl whose house has been destroyed by a missile.*

TAKE SHELTER!

The safest place during the London Blitz was outside the city. Thousands of children and elderly people were evacuated to the countryside. Some families put up tents on places like Wandsworth Common, away from target areas. The caves at Chislehurst in Kent were another popular place of safety.

Most Londoners stayed in the city. During a bombing raid they went to a specially-built bomb shelter or to a strong building. The deepest London Underground stations made the best shelters. Thousands of people went there every night with blankets, sandwiches and drinks.

The largest bomb shelters, which held hundreds of people, were huge concrete bunkers with steel doors. They had lights, toilets and shafts to let in fresh air. Better-off families built smaller concrete shelters in their gardens.

▼ 'Here you are, luv!' A waitress brings food and drink to a mother and her family sheltering from the air raids in a London Underground station.

▶ Anywhere is better than above ground – Londoners sleeping on the escalators in a crowded Underground station, October 1940.

The Government supplied more than a million do-it-yourself Anderson shelters to poorer homes. They consisted of six sheets of curved steel bolted together and placed over a shallow hole in the garden. Covered with earth (and often planted with flowers), they gave some protection against bomb blast. But the inside was damp and cold – and there was no toilet!

People also sheltered in church crypts and buildings with cellars or basements. Sandbags barricaded doors and windows above ground. Shelters protected people only from the blast of bombs falling nearby. If a shelter received a direct hit from a high-explosive bomb, most people inside were killed.

▲ 'Once upon a time . . .' Mrs Shepherd reads a goodnight story to her seven children packed into their metal Anderson shelter.

◀ An air-raid warden (and his dog, 'Rip') checks that all is well in his local air-raid shelter. Most shelters did not have proper toilets, so the smell by the end of the night was horrible!

Mrs Greenwood, who lived in Southwark, London, with her three children, remembers how frightening it was inside an Anderson shelter during an air raid:

'We listened, and huddled together as the air raid took place outside, sometimes clouds of dust came through the cracks in the doorway ". . . boy that was a close one" and the ground shook, the cups and bunks also vibrating. This sometimes went on for two, three or even four hours.'

Some believed London's preparations for the Blitz were inadequate:

'Many of Sunday night's fires in the City of London could have been avoided if fire-watching regulations had been properly observed.'

Daily Mail, Tuesday 31 December 1940

'I felt most uncomfortable about sleeping in the shelter myself and leaving the maids always in the kitchen . . . but the trouble is that Mrs B (an ambulance driver living in the house) refused to have "a great smelly maid six inches [150 mm] from her".'

From the diary of Mrs Rosemary Black

AIR RAID!

The first sign of an attack was the eerie wailing of air-raid sirens. Immediately, people turned off the lights and the gas and hurried to their places of shelter. Air-raid wardens quickly cleared the streets and made sure no lights were showing. A strange stillness fell on the city. Huddled together in their shelters, the people waited.

▶ A poster telling drivers how to prepare their cars for the black-out. Some of the instructions are about cutting the amount of light the car shows; others are about making the car difficult to steal from a darkened street.

▼ An air-raid warden, wearing a steel helmet, at the entrance to her post. The sign above her head shows that she has not lost her sense of humour!

The silence was broken by the rumble of approaching bombers. Londoners learned to tell how big a raid would be by the sound of the planes. The noise increased when the anti-aircraft guns opened up. Exploding shells and searchlights lit up the night sky like a horrible firework. Then came the bombs.

The bombs shrieked and whistled as they fell. Explosions shattered homes, shops, offices and warehouses. Fires crackled and roared. The noise carried right down to the platforms of Underground stations, where thousands of Londoners lay in the dark, listening.

Through the din came a new sound – the clanging bells of fire engines and ambulances rushing through the deserted streets. On most nights during the Blitz the dreadful clamour dragged on for hours, making it very difficult for people to sleep.

At last, the bombing stopped, the anti-aircraft guns fell silent and the drone of the aircraft faded away. Still no one went out. Only when the sirens sounded the 'all clear' did people emerge to inspect the damage that had been done to their city.

> 'My husband and I were out shopping . . . when the siren went. Well, we took no notice of it, but we were pulled into a shelter by a warden. After we'd been down there some time we heard this crash and we were all covered in dust, the whole place absolutely shook. When we came out we couldn't believe our eyes, everywhere was on fire.'

[writer unknown]

A *Daily Mail* reporter walked among the men and women watching London burning after a night raid:

> 'Every now and again you would hear someone mutter to himself: "They'll pay for this . . . ".'

31 December 1940

> '. . . there was a horrifyingly loud scream and by the time it was halfway through I was thinking it was about the longest drawn out scream I had ever heard. But it kept getting louder and louder – hateful – and after the usual horrid pause there was a long drawn out crashing. The house shook . . . like a dog coming out of water.'

From the diary of Mrs Rosemary Black

▲ London must not burn. Huge jets of water play on buildings set alight by enemy bombs during a night-time raid on 11 September 1940.

◀ All Clear! People streaming from a large London shelter after a night of air raids. Many of them are going straight from the shelter to work.

COVENTRY'S NIGHTMARE

On the moonlit night of 14–15 November 1940, the Germans bombed the Midlands city of Coventry, as well as London. The *Daily Herald* reporter F.G.H. Salisbury was one of the first people to enter Coventry the next morning:

'The cathedral is in ruins and over a large area surrounding it lies the stench of burning houses. I was told there was no let up in the noise of falling bombs, and that after a short time everyone was literally dazed by the noise.

A few miles out of Coventry, I met the first large body of refugees waking along the roadside. Children were being carried in their fathers' arms and pushed along in prams piled high with luggage.

There were suitcases and bundles on people's shoulders; little families trudged along hand in hand with rugs, blankets and anything they could save from their ruined homes.

As I walked through the ruins and dust, an old man passed me carrying a bundle of his possessions wrapped in sacking. He was mumbling to himself over and over again, "Here's a pretty how-do-you-do. Here's a pretty how-do-you-do."

I suppose he has somewhere to go.'

▼ More than 600 years of history gone in a single night. Survivors inspect the ruins of Coventry's once glorious ancient cathedral.

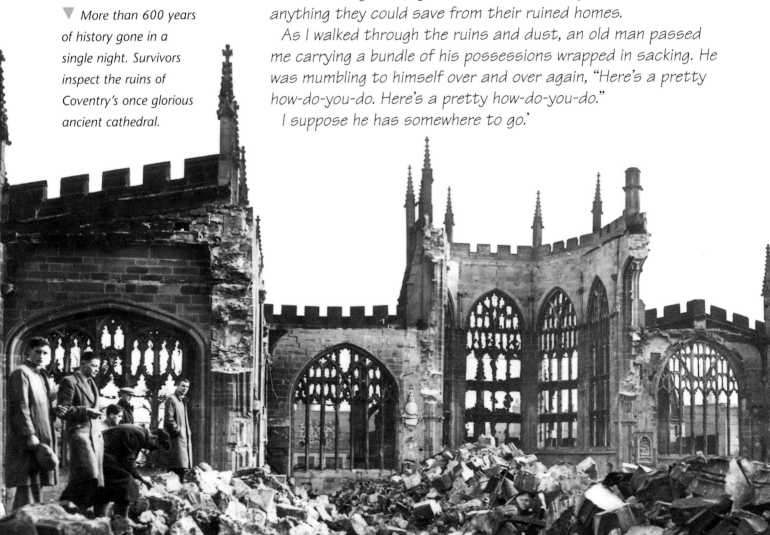

'Coventry is finished.'

A remark heard on the lips of many who survived the city's Blitz

'A nice mess, eh?'

A survivor of the Coventry Blitz

Coventry was blitzed because it was a centre of Britain's arms and machinery industry. As it was quite a small city, the 450-bomber raid caused enormous damage. Most of the city centre was destroyed, 554 people were killed and 865 were seriously wounded. However, it took only six weeks for the factories to get back to full production.

▲ *After the raid – citizens wander around the ruins of Coventry's shopping centre. The raid destroyed hundreds of beautiful old buildings.*

◄ *Survivors walk past the burned-out wreck of a bus in the centre of Coventry. At the time, the Coventry Blitz was the heaviest attack on a small city the world had ever seen.*

PICKING UP THE PIECES

The Germans dropped thousands more incendiary bombs than high-explosive bombs. As a result, fire was a much greater danger than explosion. On the night of 29 December 1940, for example, over 1,600 separate fires were burning in London alone.

Before the war, each city had its own fire service. London's was the biggest but it had nowhere near enough men or machines to cope with the Blitz – London had over 10,000 fires in the first 22 days of the Blitz. Thousands of men and women joined the Auxiliary Fire Service, which was set up to help the local brigades. Many auxiliaries had never seen a fire before – except the one in their living-room grate – so they had to learn fast.

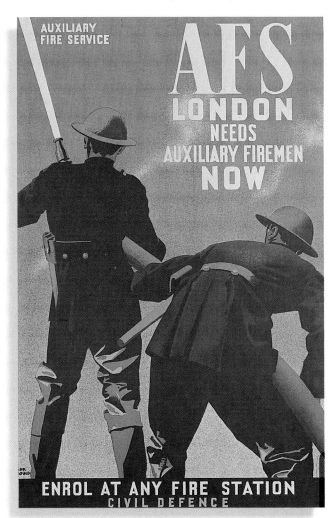

▶ *Why not become a firefighter? This poster called for volunteers to join London's Auxiliary (extra) Fire Service. During the Blitz, firefighters and fire engines came to London from all over the country.*

Other volunteers worked in rescue squads. They rescued victims trapped in buildings that had collapsed. Coal miners, expert at tunnelling, came to London to help.

When the fires were out and the injured taken away, workers moved in to repair the gas, electricity, water, telephone and postal services. It was slow, difficult work. Many homes were without electricity and running water for months.

High-explosive bombs made the firefighters' job almost impossible, as this eyewitness report of the fire in London's Surrey Docks on 7 September 1940 explains:

'The heat was so strong that wood soaked with water from firemen's hoses dried out and caught fire again. All the time, bombs fell. As they exploded they threw up great burning fragments that set alight other parts of the dock.'

Not even the Underground stations were safe from a direct hit. Sixty-four people were killed and 550 injured when a bomb fell on Balham station in October 1940. A survivor remembered,

'. . . a smell of gas and the children shouting out for their gas masks. I got my torch and flashed it up and saw water was pouring down in torrents.'

▲ *A wall map of London showing where every fire engine was. During the Blitz the map was used to make sure firefighters and machines were in the right place at the right time.*

'. . . from the many broken windows and in many half-wretched, abandoned or broken buildings and from sticks planted in bomb craters, waved Union Jacks . . . the most moving thing of the whole war.'

From the diary of Mrs Rosemary Black

◄ *A bus in the crater made by a direct hit on Balham Underground station, where many were killed.*

BEATING THE BOMBERS

Bombers came over in 'waves' of between 20 and 50 aircraft. They took off at intervals, so when one wave had dropped its bombs, the next was ready to continue the attack. Up to 700 bombers took part in a single Blitz attack.

Bombers carried between 1,000 kg and 2,000 kg of bombs. This made them quite slow. On daylight raids they were protected by 'escorts' of fighters, which flew behind and above them.

As bombers neared the British coast, 'spotters' counted them and plotted their course. At night this could not be done with the naked eye. However, Britain had a new invention – radar – which picked up approaching aircraft. This warned the Royal Air Force of an enemy attack, even at night.

▲ A Government poster encouraging everyone to help defeat the menace of enemy firebombs. 'Fritz' was a slang word for a German.

▶ Know your aircraft. The Daily Mirror produced this little booklet so that civilians could tell the difference between friendly and enemy aircraft.

As soon as bombers were spotted, fighters 'scrambled' – took off to meet them. Fighter attacks on daylight raiders were quite successful. But finding bombers and shooting at them in the dark was almost impossible.

Ground defences included barrage balloons that flew at a great height. Aircraft had to fly round them or risk getting tangled in their long trailing cables. At night bright searchlights picked out aircraft so that anti-aircraft guns could shoot at them. Anti-aircraft guns fired shells, known as 'flak', that were timed to explode at the same height as their target. They were not very accurate. One hit in every 2,000 shells was good shooting!

'Fill the balloon up with hydrogen: 30 big canisters, it took. And then float it up to about 500 feet [150 m] to get the air into the stabilisers. And then put a parachute on the cable, and fly it up to a thousand feet [300 m]. If an aircraft hit that balloon it wouldn't get back to Germany would it?'

Ann Fox

▶ *A barrage balloon rising into the air, 1944. Enemy bombers had to take care to avoid the wire cables that trailed beneath barrage balloons.*

'Chains of shells burst high in the sky, a curtain of steel. The sky must have been full of flying shrapnel.'

Daily Express, 12 September 1940, reporting the previous night's raid

◀ *ATS (Auxiliary Territorial Service) women at night action stations in west London, 1941, operating equipment that detected the height of enemy aircraft.*

THE TARGET CITIES

The Blitz had two purposes: to undermine British morale and to damage the country's communications and industry. Between September 1940 and May 1941, when the bombing was heaviest, manufacturing towns and ports were the main targets.

After the attack of mid-November 1940, Coventry was raided twice more. Seven major raids struck Birmingham. Bristol suffered major raids six times, and Manchester and Sheffield twice each. More than 800,000 homes outside London were destroyed.

To survive, Britain needed millions of tonnes of food and other supplies from overseas. In an attempt to cut this lifeline, the Germans bombed ports all round the coast. The centres of Plymouth and Swansea were completely flattened. The Clydebank area of Glasgow was bombed for four nights. Almost 2,000 people died, mostly because the bombs missed the docks and landed in crowded residential areas.

Cities targeted during The Blitz

Clydebank
Glasgow
Edinburgh
Newcastle
Sunderland
Belfast
Middlesborough
York
Hull
Manchester
Grimsby
Liverpool
Sheffield
Great Yarmouth
Nottingham
Norwich
Birmingham
Lowestoft
Coventry
Ipswich
LONDON
Swansea
Bristol
Cardiff
Bath
Canterbury
Southampton
Dover
Exeter
Portsmouth
Plymouth

▲ The ports and major British cities that were German targets during the Blitz.

▶ Fitzalan Square, Sheffield, the morning after a heavy air raid on 13 December 1940. Trams, like those at the bottom of the picture, were common in most cities at the time.

Liverpool, Cardiff, Newcastle, Belfast, Southampton and other large ports were heavily raided. Hull was bombed more than any other town in the country. The Blitz also came to smaller ports, like Lowestoft and Grimsby. Bombs destroyed or damaged 11,500 houses in Great Yarmouth. Dover was hit by bombs and by shells fired from massive guns on the other side of the English Channel.

▲ *Central Liverpool after bomb-damaged buildings had been pulled down. Many sites were not rebuilt until long after the war.*

'Twenty-one bombs fell in the most densely populated areas of the city: some of the bombers machine-gunned the ground as they passed.'

A raid on Portsmouth described by Bernard Hill in the *Daily Express*, 13 August 1940

Newspapers were not normally allowed to give the names of bombed towns in case the information helped the enemy:

'German raiders returned to the Midlands early yesterday – and lost five aircraft . . . One town had a sharp attack . . . 11 people were killed. Seven, among them a mother and her four children, were killed in a surface shelter which had a direct hit. Many incendiaries fell in fields. Fourteen pigs were killed in their sties and a clover rick . . . was destroyed.'
Daily Express, 26 June 1942

▲ *Women salvage a few treasured possessions from their bombed-out home, October 1940.*

The Blitz lasted until May 1941. There were bombing raids after that (see Canterbury on page 22) but they were not so heavy. Germany needed its planes elsewhere, and British night-fighters, fitted with radar, were better able to find and shoot down enemy raiders.

KEEP SMILING!

In 1939, when World War Two began, large-scale bombing was a new type of warfare. Experts said bombers would make city life impossible. The London Blitz was the first test of this theory.

▼ Service as usual – almost. The whole of the front of this restaurant has been covered with sandbags to protect it from bomb blasts. And the menu? 'Sandbags on toast'!

The Germans believed endless bombing would make Londoners want to surrender. Some British people feared this, too. Surprisingly, the opposite was true. The more cities were bombed, the more determined their inhabitants were to fight on. Later, the same thing happened in Germany, when German cities were bombed.

◀ The 'spirit of the Blitz'. Although this London shop has been damaged in a raid, the owner refuses to close. He has hung out flags and written a sign to let his customers know that it's business as usual.

City-dwellers felt that bombing – attacking people (especially women and children) who could not fight back – was cowardly. This bombing of civilians made them angry, not depressed. They were determined to keep their spirits up. Londoners, for example, organised sing-songs, quizzes and concerts in the Underground. Bomb-damaged shops joked about their difficulties by putting up signs reading 'More Open Than Usual'.

As everyone had to pull together to survive, community spirit was normally very strong during the Blitz. People willingly helped their neighbours, shared food and belongings, and did unpaid work. The hundreds of thousands of women who joined the Women's Voluntary Service (WVS) did vital emergency work, from driving trucks to serving in canteens.

The Government also tried to keep up morale. The speeches of Prime Minister Winston Churchill praised the people's bravery and made them feel proud of what they were doing. The BBC broadcast cheery programmes and Government posters showed the enemy as cowardly bullies.

Ron and Bunty Williamson got married as soon as war was declared. Bunty explains why:

> 'We were due to get married later, but when the war came we decided not to wait. We thought no one would survive when the bombing started, so we might as well get married right away and enjoy ourselves while we could.'

ITMA ('It's That Man Again') was the most popular wartime radio comedy show. It prompted a listener to write to the *Daily Mirror* in September 1944:

> 'Please help me enlighten my grandmother, who insists in the belief that "ITMA" is German for 'Itler's Mother.'

> 'Thinking it through, I've come to the conclusion that I'm enjoying all this in so far as it has not yet affected me personally. Doubtless I should sing a very different tune if a bomb wrecked my house or maimed me.'

From the diary of Mrs Rosemary Black

▲ Smiling WVS canteen girls bring an early morning cup of tea to women who have spent the night in a shelter.

▲ Prime Minister Winston Churchill speaks to the nation, giving his famous 'V for Victory' sign.

THE BEAUTIFUL CITIES

In 1942 British bombers attacked industrial towns in northern Germany. These towns were also historic. In response, the Germans bombed some of Britain's most famous cathedral cities. Eric Carter was in Canterbury on 1 June, the night it was first bombed.

'I woke up and thought, that's strange! All that light in a black-out. I looked out of the window and saw it was flares, great pink lights floating down from the sky. Like daylight, it was. It was so the Germans could aim their bombs.

When the bombs came I ran to my mum and we just stood there. Planes roaring and diving. The bombs made this screech, then a sort of silence, then bang! Glass smashing, plaster coming off the walls, doors coming off their hinges. And all through the cathedral clock went on chiming. It gave me hope. At least they haven't got the cathedral, I thought.

It stopped about three o'clock. The 'all clear' siren didn't sound because it had been hit, but we knew it was safe. We went out and looked about – smoke, flames, bells and the cathedral sitting in the middle of it all. Untouched.'

▲ Canterbury Cathedral survived the heavy raid on the city in June 1943. At the start of the war the cathedral's famous stained glass was removed and stored underground.

▶ Near miss! An Anderson shelter survives after the buildings around it have been blown to bits in a raid on Norwich, also a cathedral city.

'Early on Monday morning, Canterbury was subjected to a savage attack by enemy raiders, apparently as a reprisal for the bombing of Cologne the previous night. As a result many well-known buildings were destroyed by bombs or fire . . . Several of the raiders came so low that they could be seen in the moonlight.'

Kentish Gazette and Canterbury Press, 6 June 1942

◄ The misery of war. Homeless women and children pass through the streets of Canterbury as the shocked-looking men of the rescue squads look on, June 1942.

Forty-three people were killed and 97 injured in the Canterbury Blitz. In that one night, 130 high-explosive bombs and 3,600 incendiaries wiped out the centre of one of Europe's most famous old cities. York, Bath, Exeter and Norwich were smashed by similar raids. In each city hundreds of years of history vanished overnight.

'I thought, "Good Lord, the whole town has gone!" Because of all those timber houses.'

Vivienne Entwhistle, who lived in Canterbury at the time

REVENGE?

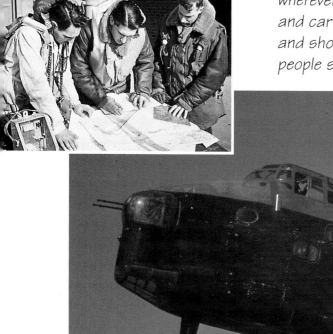

▼ Top: Planning a raid.
A British bomber crew check their course for a target German city, 1942.
Bottom: The crew of an RAF Stirling bomber leave their aircraft after a successful raid. The four-engined Stirlings were slow and made easy targets for enemy anti-aircraft defences.

Bombing was not a one-way process. Early in the war British bombers attacked Berlin and other German cities. From 1942 onwards, Allied raids were heavier and far more destructive than any launched against Britain during the Blitz. An eyewitness recalls the worst raid of all, the attack on Dresden that started on 13 February 1945:

'The alarm sounded and we hurried into our cellar which we used as an air-raid shelter. Minutes later we heard the bombers. There were non-stop explosions. Our cellar was filled with fire and smoke. The lights went out and wounded people shouted dreadfully. Terrified, we struggled to leave.

We did not recognise our street any more. Fire, only fire wherever we looked. On the streets there were burning vehicles and carts with refugees, people, horses, all of them screaming and shouting in fear of death. I saw injured women, children, old people searching for a way through ruins and flames.

We fled into another cellar overcrowded with injured and frantic people shouting, crying and praying. Suddenly the second raid began. I can't describe it! Explosion after explosion. It was beyond belief, worse than the blackest nightmare.'

An eyewitness account by Lothar Metzger, who was ten at the time of the raid

The raid on Dresden lasted for three days. Over 1,500 British and American bombers took part. We do not know how many people died: perhaps 50,000? This was more than the total number of British killed during the entire Blitz.

British newspapers tried to explain to their readers why an attack on Dresden was necessary:

'The Germans may be using Dresden – almost as large as Manchester – as their base against Koniev's [a Russian general] left flank. Telephone services and other means of communication are almost as essential to the German Army as the railways and roads which meet in Dresden. Its buildings are needed for troops and administrative services . . . [and] it has large munitions workshops.'

Evening Standard, 14 February 1945

British Bombers now attack Germany a thousand at a time!

▲ *Now it's our turn – an artist's view of a thousand-bomber raid on Germany. The raids of British and American bombers on German cities were far heavier than any launched against British cities.*

'I am now watching the Death of Germany.'

Headline in the *Sunday Pictorial,* 11 March 1945

◀ *The German city of Dresden, February 1945. Three days of intensive Allied bombing reduced the centre of the once beautiful city to a charred ruin.*

THE FLYING BOMB

By 1944 it was very difficult for enemy bombers to reach Britain without being shot down. The Germans had lost many pilots, too. However, German scientists invented the V1 – an aircraft that flew without a pilot.

This pilotless aircraft was powered by another new invention, the jet engine. It carried a one-tonne bomb. From its mobile launcher it could reach southern England. When the engine stopped, it fell to the ground and exploded.

From June 1944 onwards, 5,822 V1s landed in Britain. The attacks came as a nasty surprise. The British had believed the Blitz was over and they were terrified by the random way the V1s fell from the sky.

▲ A pilotless bomber or 'flying bomb'. German V1 missiles, like the one photographed here, were also known as 'doodlebugs' or 'buzz bombs' because of the whirring noise of their jet engines.

Almost half the V1s launched against Britain from Germany were shot down by fighters or anti-aircraft fire. But not one of the V2s, which followed, was ever brought down. The V2 was Hitler's 'miracle weapon' – a 12-metre rocket bomb with a one-tonne warhead. It travelled faster than the speed of sound and rose to a height of 80 kilometres. Fighter pilots and anti-aircraft gunners could not even see it, let alone shoot at it.

▶ The remains of a row of shops in Clapham, London, three minutes after they had been hit by a V1 missile.

◀ *A remarkable photograph of a V1 missile falling near Drury Lane, London. There was a ghastly silence just before a V1 exploded because its engine cut out over the target.*

▼ *Saved by their Anderson shelter. Two women emerge unhurt after a V1 has destroyed their home. V1 and V2 attacks came with little or no warning.*

Between September 1944 and March 1945, 1,403 V2s were launched at Britain. The attacks finally stopped only when their launch sites were destroyed or captured.

For Nan Chambers, a secretary who lived in a flat in London with her husband, the results of the V1 attacks were more tragic than the Blitz had been.

> *'I was in the kitchen preparing dinner. Reg, my husband, was in the bathroom. The doodlebug engine cut out right overhead. Silence, then – what a noise! Half the house was blown up – the half with the bathroom in it. That's how I lost my Reg.'*

The blast from a V1 exploding was enormous:

> *'One child was found dead some distance from his home, and a woman was thrown from a house and was discovered dead in another house two doors away.'*

Daily Mail, 17 June 1944

CASUALTIES AND DESTRUCTION

▼ *The news everyone had been waiting for – a selection of newspaper headlines from 29 April–5 May, 1945. Hitler killed himself on 30 April.*

▼ *Now we can get on with our lives. Standing in front of a bomb-damaged house, a group of children from Battersea, London, celebrate VE (Victory in Europe) Day, 8 May 1945.*

The Blitz brought the horrors of war to the home front. Of the 60,595 civilians killed during the war in towns and cities up and down the country, 40,000 people were killed during the Blitz. The unhappiness this caused cannot be measured, but the pain lingered on long after the war ended.

The 54,420 tonnes of bombs that fell on Britain destroyed about two million homes. The hearts of cities like Plymouth and Coventry were ripped out. Ancient cathedrals and churches were left in smoking ruins. One-third of the oldest part of London – the City – was destroyed.

The effects of the Blitz can still be seen. In cities like Exeter and Canterbury the few remaining old buildings are surrounded by new ones put up after the war. The most startling reminder of the Blitz is in Coventry, where a new cathedral has been built next to the ruins of the old one.

In some ways Britain benefited from the Blitz. Facing a common danger, people of different classes and backgrounds learned to work together. In several large cities, especially Glasgow and London, the bombs destroyed thousands of slum houses with outside toilets and no bathrooms.

The Government was forced to start a massive rebuilding programme. At first, many temporary homes (known as 'prefabs') were put up. These were gradually replaced and by the end of the 1960s most families had a chance to live in a decent home.

Victory in Europe was announced on 8 May 1945. Charles Reid of the *Daily Sketch* reported how London glowed with relief and pride.

'London was ringed with bonfires. The sky above the capital was one huge glow. It reminded one of the grim nights of London's many blitzes when the Luftwaffe had laid its trail of fires and destruction. Only last night the glow was of a different kind – the glow from a city rejoicing in victory.'

World War Two did not end with the defeat of Germany. The Japanese fought on. Only after American atomic bombs had flattened the cities of Hiroshima and Nagasaki (6 and 9 August 1945) did the Japanese emperor call on his people to surrender. The fighting finally ended on 15 August 1945 (Victory in Japan, or 'VJ' Day).

The *Daily Express* reports the dropping of the atomic bomb on Hiroshima; in a few seconds the bomb killed twice as many people as died in the Blitz:

'The city was blotted out by a cloud of dust and smoke. Sixteen hours later reconnaissance pilots were still waiting for the cloud to lift to let them see what had happened.'

7 August 1945

◄ *The Japanese city of Hiroshima after it had been hit by the world's first atomic attack on 6 August 1945. Eighty thousand people died immediately and another 60,000 within a year.*

GLOSSARY

allied Countries that fight on the same side in a war. Britain, the USA and the countries that fought on their side were called 'the Allies'.

anti-aircraft gun A gun for shooting at planes.

arms Weapons, usually small, hand-held ones.

ATS The Auxiliary Territorial Service, the women's branch of the army.

auxiliary Extra.

barrage balloon A large, gas-filled balloon that floated high in the sky to keep low-flying aircraft away.

black-out During the war all windows had to be covered so no light showed outside at night. This was called the black-out. It was done to make it harder for enemy bombers to find target cities in the darkness.

bunker An underground place of safety, usually made of concrete.

civilians Those people not in the armed forces.

crypt The basement of a church.

erase To wipe out or rub out.

evacuate To move people to a safer place.

flank The left or right side of a formation of soldiers.

Führer A German word meaning 'leader' or 'guide'. It was the title Hitler gave himself.

gas mask A mask that fits over the mouth and nose. It filters out poisonous gas in the air.

incendiary bomb A bomb that starts a fire when it lands.

Luftwaffe The German air force.

metropolis A large city area. 'The Metropolis' was London.

morale A person's mood or spirits. When people's morale is 'high' they feel cheerful and hopeful.

munitions Weapons and ammunition.

Nazi Party Germany's National Socialist Party. It was led by Adolf Hitler and followed his ideas and wishes.

radar A machine used for detecting distant metal objects, such as aircraft. The word 'radar' comes from *ra*dio *d*etection *a*nd *r*anging.

reconnaissance Scouting to find information about the enemy.

refugee Someone who flees to a place of greater safety.

residential areas Areas where people live.

sandbag A small sack filled with wet sand.

shell A large bullet that explodes when it hits its target.

shrapnel Sharp pieces of metal that fly into the air when a bomb or other missile explodes.

siren A noise-making machine.

slum A house that is not fit for people to live in.

undermine To make weaker.

warden Someone who looks after others. An air-raid warden, for example, helped people during air raids.

WVS The Women's Voluntary Service, which organised a range of wartime services, from mobile canteens to collecting scrap metal.

PROJECTS ON THE BLITZ

Write a guide to the different types of air-raid shelter, with pictures and descriptions. List the advantages and disadvantages of each.

List the different air-raid precautions, from gas masks to black-out, and illustrate them with pictures and descriptions. You might try to black out your classroom or your room at home.

A project on the Blitz needs information from *primary* and *secondary* sources. Secondary sources, mainly books and websites, are listed on the next page. They give mostly other people's views about the period of the Blitz. Primary sources come from the time of the Blitz itself, like some of the quotations in this book. They make a project really interesting and original.

Here are some ways to find primary information:
- Talking to people who lived at the time of the Blitz.

- Looking for objects remaining from the time of the Blitz. These can be large things like buildings. For example, is there an air-raid shelter still standing near you? Perhaps you have seen newer houses or shops in a row of older ones – were the new ones built to replace those destroyed in the Blitz? Smaller objects include steel helmets and gas masks.
- Visiting museums. Most local museums have excellent displays about their area during World War Two. National museums, like the Imperial War Museum in London, have a great deal of information.
- Looking at old photographs in family albums.
- Reading printed memories, like Robert Westall's, *Children of the Blitz* (Macmillan, 1995). There are many collections of old photographs, too. Ask at your local library what there is for your area.
- Visiting websites that contain primary information – but read the warning on the next page first!

FURTHER INFORMATION

BOOKS TO READ

All About the Second World War, Pam Robson (Hodder Wayland, 1996)
The Blitz, Andrew Langley (Heinemann, 1995)
Children of the Blitz, Robert Westall (Macmillan, 1995)
Coming Alive: Dear Mum, I Miss You! Stewart Ross (Evans, 2001)
Coming Alive: What If the Bomb Goes Off? Stewart Ross (Evans, 2001)
Family Life: Second World War, Nigel Smith (Hodder Wayland, 1998)
The History Detective Investigates Britain at War: Air Raids, Martin Parsons (Hodder Wayland, 1999)
History in Writing: The Second World War, Christine Hatt (Evans, 2000)
In Grandma's Day: War, Faye Gardner (Evans, 2000)
On the Trail of World War II in Britain, Alex Stewart (Watts, 1999)
What Happened Here?: Home in the Blitz, Marilyn Tolhurst and Gillian Clements (A & C Black, 2000)

... and an interesting book for older students and adults:
The Blitz, Brian Barton (Blackstaff, 1999)

WEBSITES

Just because information is on the web, it does not mean it is true. Well-known organisations like the BBC, a university or the Imperial War Museum have sites you can trust. If you are unsure about a site, ask your teacher. Here are a few useful sites to start from (all are http://www.):

angelfire.com/la/raeder/England.html
atschool.eduweb.co.uk/nettsch/time/wlife.html
bbc.co.uk/history/wwtwo.shtml
historyplace.com/worldwar2/timeline/london-blitz.htm
iwm.org.uk/lambeth/lambeth.htm

Picture acknowledgements:
The following images courtesy of the Imperial War Museum. Figures following page numbers refer to photograph negative numbers: Cover and imprint page poster: PST8382, cover (centre): HU36227, cover (background): HU1129, title page: HU49308, contents page: D280, p.4: NYT7633D, p.5: HU39714, p.6 (centre): C5423, (bottom left): HU36222, p.7 (top right): HU50146, (bottom): HU36227, p.8 (left): HU36153, (centre): HU65956, p.9 (top right): 2229182C, (centre): D5953, p.10 (centre): PST0179, (bottom left): HU36129, p.11 (top right): HU86054, (bottom): HU36145, p.12: S&G14860, p.13 (top): S&G14861, (bottom): KY1063C, p.14: PST0110, p.15 (top right): HU36128, (bottom): HU36188, p.16 (top): PST8382. (centre): extract from *Spot Them in the Air*: an aircraft identification booklet published in 1940, p.17 (top): TR1261, (bottom): TR451, p.18: HU36207, p.19 (top): HU36193, (bottom right): HU36206, p.20 (centre): HU36138, (bottom left): HU36247, p.21 (top): D2154, (bottom): PL65765, p.22: (top left) HU36192, (bottom): HU36196, p.23: KY7025C, p.24 (left): TR134, (centre): TR9, p.25 (top right): PST0734, (bottom): HU3321, p.26 (left): HU36294, (bottom): HU36166, p.27 (top): HU636, (bottom): HU635, p.28 (left): HU87435, (bottom): HU49308, p.29: IND5219.

Map artwork on page 18 by Tim Mayer

Sources of quoted material
Pages 6 (Doreen Wilkinson), 9 (Mrs Greenwood), 21 (Ron and Bunty Williamson), 22 (Eric Carter) and 27 (Nan Chambers): Personal interviews with author
Pages 7, 9, 11, 15 and 21: The diary of Rosemary Black cited in *The War Papers* no.11, Peter Way and Marshall Cavendish Partworks Ltd., London, 1976
Page 11: Unknown writer cited in Caroline Lang, *Keep Similing Through: Women in the Second Word War*, CUP, Cambridge, 1989, p.15
Page 13 (2nd quote): Cited in the *Daily Herald*, 16 November 1940
Page 15 (1st quote): Cited in *Ourselves in Wartime*, Odhams, London, p.75
Page 15 (2nd quote): Cited in *The War Papers* no.12, Peter Way and Marshall Cavendish Partworks Ltd., London, 1976
Page 17: Ann Fox cited in Mavis Nicholson, ed., *What Did You Do in the War, Mummy?*, Chatto and Windus, London, 1995, p.78
Page 23: Vivienne Entwhistle cited in Anne Pope, ed., *Memories of the Blitz*, Canterbury City Council Museums, 1992
Pages 24-25: Taken from www.timewitnesses.org

INDEX